anythink

Food Field Trips

Let's Explore
Pumpkins!

Jill Colella

Lerner Publications ◆ Minneapolis

Hello, Friends,

Everybody eats, even from birth. This is why learning about food is important. Making the right choices about what to eat begins with knowing more about food. Food literacy helps us be curious about food and adventurous about what we eat. In short, it helps us discover how delicious the world of food can be.

Goodbye, summer. Hello, fall! Round, orange pumpkins are waiting to be picked. Fall fruits and vegetables such as pumpkins, squash, and apples are fresh ingredients for fall cooking. I like eating roasted squash with maple syrup on it.

For more inspiration, ideas, and, recipes, visit www.teachkidstocook.com.

Jill

About the Author

Happy cook, reformed picky eater, and longtime classroom teacher Jill Colella founded both *Ingredient* and *Butternut*, award-winning children's magazines that promote food literacy.

Lerner Publications Company
An imprint of Lerner Publishing Group, Inc.
241 First Avenue North
Minneapolis, MN 55401 USA

For reading levels and more information, look up this title at www.lernerbooks.com.

Main body text set in Mikado. Typeface provided by HVD.

Library of Congress Cataloging-in-Publication Data

Names: Colella, Jill, author.
Title: Let's explore pumpkins! / by Jill Colella.
Description: Minneapolis : Lerner Publications, [2020] | Series: Food field trips | Includes bibliographical references and index. | Audience: Age 4–8. | Audience: K to Grade 3.
Identifiers: LCCN 2019011159 (print) | LCCN 2019014628 (ebook) | ISBN 9781541581791 (eb pdf) | ISBN 9781541563049 (lb : alk. paper)
Subjects: LCSH: Pumpkin—Juvenile literature.
Classification: LCC SB347 (ebook) | LCC SB347 .C65 2020 (print) | DDC 635/.62—dc23

LC record available at https://lccn.loc.gov/2019011159

Manufactured in the United States of America
1-46466-47543-8/8/2019

SCAN FOR BONUS CONTENT!

Table of Contents

Picture Glossary

fall

farm

leaf

seed

soup

ALL ABOUT PUMPKINS

Pumpkin can be tasty to eat. The fleshy part of a pumpkin can be boiled, steamed, baked, or roasted.

Soup, pasta, curry, and even sweet foods such as pies and muffins can have pumpkin in them.

Pumpkin seeds can be eaten too! When toasted in the oven, the seeds become crunchy. Eat them as a snack, or add them to a soup or salad.

LET'S COMPARE

Pumpkins belong to a group of vegetables called squash. Squash comes in many shapes, sizes, and colors. You can cut it into chunks and roast it. You can mash it or bake it whole.

Zucchini squash is long, green, and soft inside.

Acorn squash has dark green skin and hard flesh. It has stringy pulp in it.

Butternut squash is tall and orange with hard flesh and seeds.

Delicata squash has thin skin. When cut into rings, the shape of a flower appears.

Hubbard squash looks like a bumpy, green pumpkin.

Kabocha squash is dark green. It is the sweetest of all squashes.

LET'S EXPLORE

The inside of a pumpkin has pulp in it. Pulp feels soft and stringy. Tangled in the pulp are pumpkin seeds.

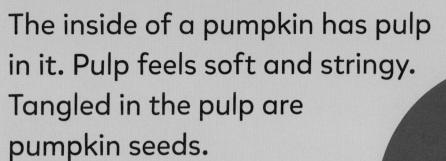

What do you think the inside of a pumpkin feels like?

9

Pumpkins are planted in the summer. Pumpkin seeds grow into shoots and roots. The shoots and roots grow into large plants before small pumpkins appear.

seed

seed

shoot

roots

leaves

shoot

roots

PICKING PUMPKINS

Let's visit a farm with a pumpkin patch! A pumpkin patch is a field where pumpkins grow.

We need to pick the perfect pumpkin for carving. Pumpkins are ready to be picked in the fall.

How do you know when it is fall?

How are these things the same or different?

What do you see at the farm?

This farm has a rooster, a tractor, piglets, and apples.

There is also a pumpkin patch. The pumpkins are ready to be picked!

What shape are the pumpkins?
Count how many pumpkins you see.

The pumpkins are hidden under big green leaves and curly vines. Pumpkin leaves are soft. Pumpkin vines are prickly and rough.

Have we found
our pumpkin yet?

Yes! It is big, round,
and very heavy!

What color and shape would your perfect pumpkin be?

We need to find an adult to help us lift the pumpkin.

It's time to take our pumpkin home!

LET'S COOK

Remember to always have an adult present when cooking in the kitchen!

PUMPKIN SOUP

INGREDIENTS

- 3 tablespoons (42.5 g) butter
- 1 medium onion, finely chopped
- 1 cup (250 g) applesauce
- 2 cups (236.5 mL) vegetable broth
- ½ cup (120 mL) water
- 1 can (15 ounces, or 425 g) cooked canned unsweetened pumpkin
- ¼ teaspoon ground nutmeg
- ¼ teaspoon ground black pepper
- 1 can (12 ounces, or 340 g) evaporated milk

1. Melt butter in a saucepan over medium heat.

2. Add onion and cook until soft.

3. Add all the other ingredients except evaporated milk and stir.

4. Turn heat to medium-high and bring the mixture to a boil.

5. Reduce heat to low, and cook for 15 minutes.

6. Add half of the evaporated milk. If soup is too thick, add the remaining evaporated milk.

7. Spoon the soup into bowls and enjoy.

SEE THIS RECIPE IN ACTION!

LET'S MAKE

Use a pumpkin to make a feeder for backyard friends. Always have an adult present when you are working with sharp objects!

PUMPKIN SQUIRREL FEEDER

MATERIALS

- butter knife or pumpkin carving kit
- 1 small or medium pumpkin
- large spoon

1. Cut off the stem of the pumpkin to make an opening.

2. Hollow out a pumpkin with the spoon, remove the pulp, and set the seeds aside.

3. Carve circles, squares, or triangles into your pumpkin. Make sure the carvings are big enough for squirrels to climb in and out.

4. Place seeds back inside, and put the top back on the pumpkin.

5. Place your feeder where you can easily see squirrels feasting!

Let's Read

Agriculture in the Classroom
http://agintheclassroom.org/TeacherResources/AgMags.shtml

Lindeen, Mary. *I Pick Fall Pumpkins*. Minneapolis: Lerner Publications, 2017.

Midwest Giant Pumpkin Growers
http://www.midwestgiantpumpkingrowers.com/

Owings, Lisa. *From Pumpkin to Pie*. Minneapolis: Lerner Publications, 2015.

The Pumpkin Patch
http://pumpkin-patch.com

Rustad, Martha E. H. *Fall Pumpkin Fun*. Minneapolis: Lerner Publications, 2019.

Photo Acknowledgments

Image credits: vewfinder/Shutterstock.com, p. 1; Brian Mollenkopf/Getty Images, p. 3 (fall); Brian A Wolf/Shutterstock.com, p. 3 (farm); Shi Zheng/EyeEm/Getty Images, p. 3 (leaf); lovelyday12/Shutterstock.com, p. 3 (seed); kivoart/Getty Images, p. 3 (soup); istetiana/Getty Images, p. 4; ALLEKO/Getty Images, p. 5 (soup); Mark Pendergrass/EyeEm/Getty Images, p. 5 (seed); Elena Veselova/Shutterstock.com, p. 5 (pie); Dawn LeFever/Shutterstock.com, p. 6; Ariel Skelley/Getty Images, pp. 7 (kid), 12 (left); Anna Kashkanov/EyeEm/Getty Images, p. 7 (leaves); Smileus/Shutterstock.com, p. 7 (pumpkin); georgeclerk/Getty Images, p. 8 (chicken); Mint Images/Getty Images, p. 8 (tractor); Bruno Guerreiro/Getty Images, p. 8 (pigs); tomeng/Getty Images, p. 8 (apples); J Michael Fitzpatrick/Shutterstock.com, p. 9; Malcolm P Chapman/Getty Images, p. 10; Eag1eEyes/Shutterstock.com, p. 11 (pumpkins); Cat Act Art/Shutterstock.com, p. 11 (flower); ZenShui/Laurence Mouton/Getty Images, p. 11; Cavan Images/Getty Images, p. 12 (right); Jose Luis Pelaez Inc/Getty Images, p. 13; Andersen Ross Photography Inc/Getty Images, p. 14; Stephan Fenzl/EyeEm/Getty Images, p. 15; Shyripa Alexandr/Shutterstock.com, p. 16 (zucchini); Elliotte Rusty Harold/Shutterstock.com, p. 16 (butternut); Amy J Kamps/Getty Images, p. 16 (acorn); Mark Herreid/Getty Images, p. 17 (delicata); cislander/Getty Images, p. 17 (Hubbard); sdstockphoto/Getty Images, p. 17 (kabocha); Denise Torres/Shutterstock.com, p. 18; Laura Westlund/Independent Picture Service, pp. 10, 23; Westend61/Getty Images, p. 20; Chubykin Arkady/Shutterstock.com, p. 21; C. Hamilton/Shutterstock.com, p. 22.

Cover: Jodie Witmer/Shutterstock.com (pumpkins); Jose Luis Pelaez Inc/Getty Images (holding); Cavan Images/Getty Images (picking); GMVozd/Getty Images (pie); Jeremiah Schumacher/Getty Images (back).

Disney Moana THE MIGHTY MAUI MAKES A FRIEND

By

KALIKOLEHUA HURLEY

Illustrated by

MEHRDAD ISVANDI

A special thanks to the wonderful people of the **PACIFIC ISLANDS** for inspiring us on this journey as we bring the world of Moana to life.

To my mom, the mightiest of them all. And to my love, CLK.

–KH

I dedicate this book to my wife, Sara, for all her support.

–MI

LOS ANGELES · NEW YORK

Designed by Tony Fejeran

Printed in the United States of America

First Hardcover Edition, February 2017   10 9 8 7 6 5 4 3 2 1

ISBN 978-1-4847-8292-7

FAC-03427-17006

Library of Congress Control Number: 2016953972

For more Disney Press fun, visit www.disneybooks.com

For more Moana fun, visit www.disney.com/moana

Let me tell you a story about the mighty Maui. You've heard of him, right?

Half man, half myth. **ALL HERO.**

Well, today must be your lucky day, because that hero is

Me, Maui:
The Greatest

demigod in the Pacific. With my magical fishhook, I've done

INCREDIBLE THINGS.

I PUSHED UP
the sky so humans could walk upright.

I SLOWED DOWN
the
sun

so people could get
MORE WORK DONE.

and even helped **CREATE** coconuts!

Yeah,
YOU'RE WELCOME.

Oh, and I can also change my shape.

Supercool
SHARK?
Coming right up.

AWESOME GIGANTIC HAWK?

Thought you'd never ask.

Itsy-bitsy also

AWESOME BUG?

Done! So watch where you step!

I used to live
on my very own
private island,

Being alone
wasn't so bad.
I didn't have to share my
dinner. I could tell
myself my favorite story
a Million times.

(PS: It was about me.)

But one day, I realized there was one
thing the mighty Maui had yet to do:

BE A FRIEND. . . .

Then Moana showed up, and it was

Naturally, I became an expert at being **A FRIEND.**

And I found out some of friendship's most mysterious rules right away.

For example, it turns out friends have to be **NICE** to each other.

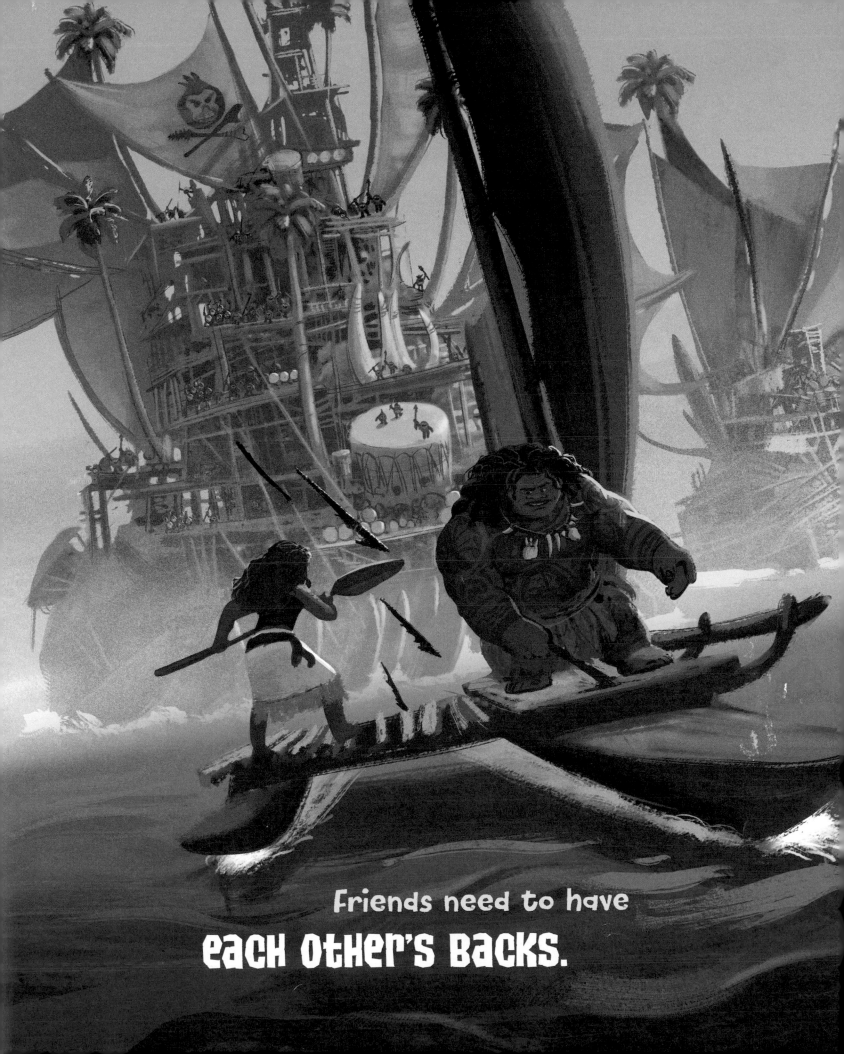

Friends need to have
EACH OTHER'S BACKS.

And when the going gets tough, friends never, ever leave each other **STRANDED.**

In no time, I was becoming the greatest friend of all time.
You see, friends teach each other new things—
like me teaching Moana how to be the world's
SECOND-BEST WAYFINDER.

FRIENDS SHARE.
Hey, when you're a master
fisherman, you can spare
a fish or two.

FRIENDS LISTEN.

Between us, even a demigod
who has experienced it all can
discover something new.

Having a friend means you've got someone to

CHEER YOU ON.

It also means you have someone who accepts **YOU FOR YOU.** I learned that from Moana.

Moana and I,
together as friends,
went on an epic adventure
and basically **SAVED**
THE WORLD.

And the mighty Maui finally added **FRIENDSHIP** to his list of feats.

Thanks for listening to my story.
Now you can call yourself

MY
FRIEND,
too.